Vuoto Rain

Eleanor Lee

ISBN: 978-1-4907-7211-0 (sc)
         978-1-4907-7210-3 (e)

Library of Congress Control Number: 2016905005

Trafford rev. 04/19/2016

 www.trafford.com

North America & international
toll-free: 1 888 232 4444 (USA & Canada)
fax: 812 355 4082

In Memory of Giovanni Batista Gurrieri Jr

A special thanks to Kizzy Nadal for being God's vessel and helping me find my salvation because of you I found life and had the courage to write this book. I'm so blessed to have a mentor like you.

Eleanor Lee

Author's letter:

Dear Reader,
Thanks for your interest in this book. I have put together a collection of poems that I wrote through my life during very hard times, heart breaking moments and my journey to find my spiritual self. The tough moments are the ones that bring you to your knees, and force you to find a higher power. It does not matter what religion or beliefs you have this book is about a spiritual journey that I want to share with you poetically.
Hope you enjoy this book

Table of Contents

Gone

Relieved or depressed,
Deceived or repressed.
Confessions of my confused soul
Reflections in her face of him.
Collections of memories
   flow through my head,
Like a rushing waterfall.
The dread of telling them,
Preparing them for
   the rain to fall.
The tall lingering look,
She'll see me with when her
   heart starts to weep.
Bereaved and betrayed,
Sensations of temptations
   flow through my head.
Perpetually
   profound pieces of me that don't fit.
His rebellious soul foretold my future.
My heart scattered and shattered.
My head desperate and destructive.
He's gone never to return again.
Completely consumed by my fears and tears.
The pain prays on my brain,
An evil drains my vain.
Stains of his memory press on word,
Like waves in the ocean.
If the pain pushes,
My soul will fade,
Ill lose my strength to pray.

Eleanor Lee

One Day

Some of us may be a little more hard headed than thee,
But give us time and one day you will see how quickly we
Have learned to take a knee
One day you will see

Beauty in the Beast

As I take a walk in the fresh spring air a man walk past me with wild hair.
I catch a glimpse of his crazy stare it seems to tear through me without a care.
An unsettling chill runs across my skin.
My awkwardness beings to spin and my breath thins.
My body has frozen and the dark grows close.
A full dose of his horrid ghost seeps in me.
I want to flee in search of glee, but I can't my mind rants on about the binds it finds me in.
My soul is navigating blind aligned with this unkind design.
NO I say you will not break me, you will not take my light.
Somethings not right I can't fight against him.
Suddenly I can see through the black hole that is him.
Within this trolls pile of coal lays a soul?
I will touch the cold beast with my warming heart.
I part from my fear and start to look deep into this misunderstood beast.
I seep through his unguarded cracks and coat his crippled heart with a thin layer of love.
Soon the ruff sandy heart of the beast transforms.
Suddenly the whistle of fierce fall winds rapidly rip the unwanted substance away.
I begins to pray lord help this creature.
I will stay till I see rays of faith appear this day and shine.
I will never retreat, than repeat again and again until this seed grows bright like the beautiful
Moonlight turns thee scary dark into amazing blue beauty.
It's my duty to help him pull through and pursue a better existence.
Perfect persistence will propel a perfect pastel shell.
As the darkness sheds we bid farewell.
A spark in me I see as a grin spreads on his face.

I see such beauty fill the space were death was laced.
Beauty was found in this beast with a little unconditional love I see.
Now he is freed.
Time to spread your glow so the rest of the world can feed.

It Left With Yesterday

A barrowed feeling of sorrow.
Feeling that will last through tomorrow.
A realization:
It dose not pay to wallow.
Stand up,
Swallow and breathe,
Read between the lines,
There's hope on the finest line.
Hope for dieing binds in my heavy mind.
Stop,
Rewind,
Life dose not have to be this way.
A ray of hope I see it has not yet faded away.
Today is the begin of tomorrow,
The sorrow left with yesterday.

In This Place

In this place,
This place within.
I can feel my skin crawl through the night.
I try to put up a fight,

But the lack of breath in me,
Soon is the death of me?
The power I don't feel will drag out the hours.
My nerves begin to scream.

The gleam of light has not yet been seen.
The beat is still thumping hard,
As hard as the bumping in my heart.
I sought for wisdom.
Wisdom from the thought that over power my soul,
But nothing was found.
Nothing but aggressions,
Aggressions of bears:
I can't find anyone,
Anywhere.

Still strongly leads

Uncontrollable thoughts of you releases cries of prayer rushing from my soul.
Over-whelming memories hold me like a prisoner they won't let me go.
Silent hope drains from my rainy brain.
Sudden clutter start to gain.
I need shelter from the whining and weary storms.
Be my ancer through the whistling winds.
Let my touch satisfy your starving soul.
I can breathe passion into your veins.
You are the blood that strains to circulate though me.
But the belligerent bellows from below my feet bombard my senses steering me from you.
Their frantic whales frighten me.
Loud ferocious shrieks send shudders shooting up my thighs.
My lungs fill with sighs and goosebumps blanket my skin.
Remote fear crowd the blessed glow I've been given.
Interpreting my spirits desire becomes unobtainable.
Agony seems to blend with my blood like the rain intertwines with the river.
My feet go numb and fade away.
Running is impossible now.
My breath shortens and slows slightly stealing sensation securely stashed in my soul.
Darkness invades my sight and devours all the light.
Without my glowing light my passions will start flowing from the darkness that embodied my eyes.
My adapting brain narks on my heart and reveals its untainted remains.

The heart is undamaged ad thriving.
It released a comforting warmth as soothing as the sunrays shining
   thought the tree tops and gently touching my raised face.
This moment of silent chaos murmurs little musical nots in my ear,
Suddenly I hear:

> **"Dry your tears and quiet your fear,**
> **A right heart will never disappear.**
> **Tho buried and dirtied by trouble**
> **Deeds this heart still strongly leads.**
> **Greed may be used as fertilizer,**
> **But on this the heart dose not feed"**

My fearless heart starts to awaken like a sleeping giant.
A harmonious power begins reaping the fears that are unjustly keeping my senses detained.
Rapidly being purged of unsettling emotions,
Reuniting my soul and spirit.
I am not freed a faithful heart has guided me.
Now I clearly see who has been placed hear just for me.
The sight of your face has tinted my skin red.
The pace of the beat of my heart speeds.
Your hypnotizing eyes leaves small seeds sowed in me.
Fear swiftly seduced sections of my.
But your phenomenal light conquer
   fear and released me.
When you touch me the frightening cries quiet
   and my guiding light and I are reunited.
As the night passed as the fight comes to an end.
As our light become one we sing:

> **"Tho buried and dirtied by troubled deeds**
>   **These hearts still strongly lead"**

Now you and I are free to flee though
   the tree tops into the sunset

Eleanor Lee

And across the sea.
A new land I see so many beautiful creatures made just for me.
As we glide through our newly formed world,
Big hopes and dreams quickly fill me.
Will power conquered the cypher of clever despair.
As we star at our marvelous new atmosphere we create a collision
Of pure love and care.
A superior seduction flows from our bodies like smoke from my lips.
We have tamed the untamable.
We repaired the ruins that flooded our faith.
Together we killed the skilled guild of rotten thoughts and evil knots
On our heart.
Now the rain has come and the chain of stains the pain has laid are
Washing away.
The decade braid of tainted sued flesh that hangs from my head has
Turned to clay.
So I stay pray wait and give way for the day he is done molding me
In a flawless way.
That's when we will see nothing but beautiful rays of light.
Than our night will become filled spectacular sights of untold dreams,
While bold colors illuminated from the clouds between.

Maze of Days

Hunger,
The starvation of the soul,
The sweet morning resurrection of impeccable hurt.
Horrific nights waking up in screams.
I try to fight the fight but,
It's never what it seems.
There's hope in the darkest times.
Just look for the light that shines bright.
What's right will soon prevail.
That nails that bind my troubles to me,

Never seem to fail.
The grudges I hold,
Never seem to fade.
The days I have left,
Set the better haze above my maze of days.
The glaze that hides my eyes from this hazy maze,
Will soon fade away.
So I can get back to my life right away.
No more maze of days,
Cause my ways has changed.
The brittle choice that affects my ways,
The glaze will soon be laid away.
For the rest of my days,
In this maze of ways.
Payment will come to all,
No matter how hard you crawl.
So better your ways,
We don't have many days.

Over-Come

Obstacles arise,
Like prizes to be won.
The kind that none can over-come.
Lies rise,
They make my heart hurt and my eyes cry.
The love I've lost,
The ridicule I've suffered.
Like a tide,
I can rise above them all,
Even when I fall.
I fear what I don't know,
It will become clear.
As I stare thought the glass...

With a raspy voice I say;
'Like a tide,
I can rise above them all'.
Dignity can shackle me down like a slave.
Stationary waves dig my early grave,
Because I have misbehaved.
Brave and weary burdens come to save me.
I stop to gaze upon the life he gave me.
It hits me,
Like sunstroke...
Like a tide I can rise and over-come.

Lost Time

I think about the lost time.
What has it cost me?
Flee from the key to an eternal guarantee.
It kept my unkind mind blind.
Here and now,
I make a vow,
Fearlessly steer clear...
Of that sinful spheres.
True new views of less hazy ways.
My children have suffered because of my selfish ways.
Nights for them are due for light.
So their sight can grow bright.
And...
Invite delightful dreams,
That might ignite what's right.
Maybe their eyes will cry no more.
I rest my blessed upon my breast.
Unconditional love...
Unbelievable...
Marvelous...

Fabulous love from my blessing to me.
When it gets to hard...
Take a deep breath and pray,
Than soon you'll see
Afternoon sky turning to night.
Snow glistening in the sun.

Draining silence

This unbearably loud silence is killing me.
The lack of noisy crowds scream at me.
All the life seems to be at my back, keeping me off balance and knocking me off track.
Stillness is seeping out of every pore in my body.
Even the howling winds produce no speed to soar.
I open up my mouth to let out a roar but still no sound.
All words have ravished the core of me. Left nothing but an empty shell of me.
I think I fell into a silent hell.
When I blink I can feel myself sink further into this soundless cell.
My memories now seem like visions from another life.
I'm trapped I cry a loud cry for help.
Capped off, unreleased to tease the wild in me.
Un-freed bound like a caged canary.
This obsessive aggression is spreading like a wildfire.
It's perspiring through my pore soiling my attire.
As the climax of silence arrives the alliance of kindness quickly subsides.
In the distance I see mental suicide rushing at me and he has demonic eyes.
I try to rise above him but the toxic tonic he brings chronically keeps me sipping.
The corrosive caustic narcotic is stripping me of my cosmic logic.
Soon my knowledge is stolen, depleted and drained from my brain.
Nothing is being gained staying chained stained and trained.
This black hole will soon consume me if I don't break free from this old cold mold.

Life Changing Effect

Every change in life leaves a scare on your soul.
Every switch leaves an un-repaired mark.
Every friend you leave,
Leaves a tear on your pillow.
To have an unscarred soul,
Is to have never been born.
Change alters who you are,
Without snatching the best of you.
Every problem that arises is a lesson,
Every solution is a pattern to be followed.
Every pattern is a decision to be made.
A decision made alters life.
There are no bad alterations.
Belief that you make your own pattern,
Relief,
That the pattern you run can still be changed
Not to be bought,
Not to be caught,
To live life the best way you know how.
Be proud of the amazing being you are.
To run your pattern a day at a time,
Don't let life run the pattern for you.
Life is sacred,
We only live it once,
So cherish what you have,
Instead of what you don't.
Condoning depression is a waste.
Pace yourself...
Lay back.
Rest.
Enjoy what you have,
Some may not be so lucky.

Life's choices

Binding my emotions.
Riding them,
Through the fluttery consecutive waves of life.
Life's slave for tormented emotions.
When will the light appear?
The light will help steer through,
The fluttery waves.
Life's choices,
Soon it becomes...
Utterly impossible to see through them.
Choices crash down on me,
Like a tone of bricks.
It becomes our choice,
To build with them,
Or get built by them.

In All of Us

I want to pass to the side with golden grass.
I'm ready to surpass this stage of fragile glass.
He will mend all my shattered pieces.
The pain he releases.
When I'm leaven to go to heaven...
My true and new self will be freed.
My eyes are the windows to my stained soul.
I'm waiting for my spiritual awakening.
A non-fictional image would make my spirit shine.
An angel all mine.
Endless amount of time with someone so divine.
His kind hands catch me when I fall.
Above all...
I cannot hide behind my bearing walls,

He sees me all in all.
His love for me is never discrete...
It is concrete and always complete.
His love warms my smile.
He is in all of us.

Lose of a child

A tragedy,
As tragic as a tornado.
An emotional experience,
That I'll never overcome.
The loss of my child has ripped my heart out through my throat.
A stomach clenching feeling.
It starts from my head,
Moves through my body like a forest fire.
I admire the strong,
They thrive to survive
After an over whelming experience.
Deliverance is a need.
A mother attaches to her child,
Like a bird catches the wind.

The Drag down

Love,
It's like a dove in flight,
It is always right.
I wish I felt it with all my might,
See it with all my sight,
I want to feel as high as a kite,
I want to sore like I use to.
Feel the passion,
Not the depression.

I want out of this two-way dimension.
It struck me hard when the bars shut,
I'm all alone,
A long way from home.
My family hurts,
I wish I could take back the bad.
My eyes become redder,
My heart becomes harder,
My soul begins to fade,
It's too late,
I've sunk to the bottom.
The air in my lungs begins to fade,
My heart slows to a light thump,
My eyes become heavy.
Skin becomes cold,
Body becomes old.
I hit the ground.
I feel the sand on my cold pale skin.
The water is all around me.
As my hair flutters with the waves,
I realize that my heart, mind and soul have completely gone away.
Depression has taken its toll on me,
To redeem me for my sins.
No more grins,
No more nothing.
Just depression.
Redemption for my thought,
Redemption for my feelings,
Redemption for being me.
I believe I have paid for my sins,
By living here,
At the bottom of the sea.

Eleanor Lee

I Need You More

Without you,
Fusion with evil is my destiny.
I can't love without you,
I can't make it above.
I need you more.
When you're not with me,
My mind runs and evil comes.
When you don't talk to me,
I stray and hide like pray.
I think I need you more.
If you leave me,
My life would be a lie,
Then I will die.
If you leave,
Nothing would matter,
Than my heart will shatter.
I think I need you more.
When I sing,
I sing for you.
When I breathe,
I breathe because of you.
I think I need you more.

My Father's Eyes

In my fathers eyes,
I am great.
I have the perfect faith,
Walking through that gate with out hate.
In my fathers eyes,
I hide no lies.
Mistakes I partake in are forgiven,

In my fathers hand he keeps me,
He understands my faith is firm like land.
Not grainy like sand.
In my fathers hands he shelters me.

I Love You

When I see you,
I want to smile,
Even if it's only for a short while.
When we touch,
I can feel my blood rush.
My heart pounds,
My face gets all-flush.
Time comes to a stop.
Hearts chime in-sink.
Your hearts thump I hear.
Down your face rolls one tear.
I love you my dear but,
If I blink it might all disappear?
I fall so deep in your eyes.
When you're around there's nothing I could hide.
There are no words,
For how you make me feel inside.
To be your bride would be a dream.
Streams of love bust through my seams.
I never thought I could feel like I do.
How can I explain how much I love you?
In my dreams I see it so clear.
WE will be together for the rest of our years.

I won't fall

I've had a lot of temptation and trial in my life,
But I'm done walking down that mile.
Piles of hurt have sat on heart.
Time to part from hate,
Then walk through the right gate.
Now I'm free,
The light that shine bright in me.
The whole world can see,
What change done for me?
I'm breaking free from the chains that hold me down.
I felt cold when the world turned her back on me,
I got to find godliness,
So the next time the devils calls...
I won't fall.
I'm tired of feeling short,
It's time to feel tall.
I've been lead around by people with fake crowns.
When inside their nothing but undercover Clowns.
With feelings that only make them frown.
Change is coming around.

That sounds so nice.
It's time for change to come around.
The range of danger will progress in an instant.
Persistence consisting of violence.
Change is upon us.

My Little Angles

My fears bind me down.
Tears will not fall this time around.
I've found that special thing to hold on to.
That something makes the cold pass on.

My little Angles
The feeling of falling on my face is rising.
This feeling is powerful that's not surprising.
I feel I have to disguise myself,
Walk with stealth.
My little Angels
Fear is feeling up the fold in my soul.
My cold nights are soon to grow.
That freshness chips away the ice in my soul.
I find myself staying away.
M little Angles

Shattered thoughts

Imprisonment,
A process of belief.
An un-intended reaction,
Purity,
As pure as an unborn child.
A sign of caution,
A one-way street,
To believe and never go back.
My faith,
It's in the hands of the lord.
Hope to someday,
See what has never been seen,
To feel what's' never been felt.
Smell unbelievable fragrances,
Touch what has never been touched.
Taste what has never been imagined,
To feel the passion that is unimaginable.
A prize that's priceless.
Arise and sing,
The restless noise of sorrow

A bellow for the forbidden life.
Noxiousness,
For the narcotic that rapes my mind.
A bind in my soul,
The glow has been lock away,
To stay away,
No more play.
A tray of awkwardness,
No more rebounds left.
A titan's wave of terror for torment.
A raving idolization,
A spiritual awakening,
A soft touch of a blessing from the lord.
Up roared in happiness.
Blessing the blessed in bliss to kiss his hand.
A longing for guidance from someone supreme.
Redeem myself in his eyes,
No more lies, no more tears I can't cry.
A dead spirit fades and a joyful one is resurrected.
A view and perception that only I understand,
Like a fierce untamed dagger piercing through my cold pale skin.
As time flies past me I feel colder and colder and more alone.
As if I were the only one inhabiting this ferocious planet.
An unstable bond hoping to be broken.
Awakened I realize,
Thoughts are bleeding the heart.
I part from my old ways and look forward to better days.
Among the best,
I lay them to rest,
To test the less fortunate.
To stand before god with strong faith.

Perfect Place

A perfect place.
Some say there's no such thing.
No such place with harmony.
Places with out hate.
A place where true love thrives through.
In my mind,
In my heart,
In my soul.
I know other wise.
Somewhere true love exists in total bliss.
The Holy Ghost in me says if I walk the righteous path.
When the time comes,
If my faith is still strong,
Nothing will stand between my
    perfect place and me.

Praise

You died for us?
Than we will drop to one knee.
We know you will never forsake us.
Through your eyes we can truly see.
You keep us safe for that,
I will give you glory.
We want your grace to surround us.
You found us crying on the ground.
Forgive us for the sins of our flesh.
With you we can breathe fresh.
Use us for your vessel lord.
You have restored us.
You finish my masterpiece.
You have released us from our sins.
Because of you we live.
SO today we praise you.

Eleanor Lee

His Love

As I lay at night,
I pray.
Will you watch over me?
Use all your sight.
I do nothing right.
When things start to get too hard,
You are there to put strength in me.
You make me truly believe.
You're always there to help.
When my troubles get to heavy to hold,
You hold them for me.
When my heart grows cold,
You become my blanket.
When I lose my breath,
You breathe for me.
You're always there to help.
When I lose my sight,
You lend me your eyes.
When I can't hear,
You become my ears.
When I have no one to talk to,
You become my counselor.
AT time i feel no one loves me,
Then you wrap your arms around me.
You're always there to help.
When I begin to fall,
You are there to catch me.
At night when I try not cry,
You come to wipe my tears.
When my soul start to darken,
You shine a light.
When I begin to lose faith in you,
You hold me tight.

I know you are my true promise,
JESUS!!!
You're always there to help.
Thank you for believing in me,
Even when I don't believe in you.

His Arms

The best,
He knows.
Blessings he has bestowed.
When he put me upon his breast,
The stress moves on,
Then I feel blessed.
When I pray to stay out of harms way,
I can lie safely in his arms.
His ray helps me find my way.
He carries me through...
Tedious temptations raiding my brain.
With out him I would fail,
When the hail started to fall.
My hollow soul will fallow him anywhere.
Just as the bellow of the willow...
Fallows the wind.

Pray About It

Time is spent,
Day is at its end.
The sun is asleep,
The moon is at its peak.
The stars come out to play.
Before I lay my head down,
I begin to pray.

Eleanor Lee

I understand I have to pay for my actions.
The reactions to my anger.
But danger stands in my way.
My straight path has gone astray.
Warn days turn cold.
My heart is weeping,
And my soul is bleeding.
Where's the gleam of light I used to see.
I still feel week.
So today I pray to you like never before.
I need faith!
I need strength!
I need you.
AMEN!!!

My Dad

He makes me feel bad,
With out saying a word.
I've heard every word he said,
Shhhh......
He's my dad
He appreciates the smallest things I do.
My wings he pruned and trimmed so they would grow.
He's my dad
The grinch grin he gives when he's been sneaky.
His cheeky personality.
That's my dad.
The way he says,
I love you...
Most lovingly.
When my gray days have drawn me astray,
He was always there,
To help me find my way.

He's my dad.
He is a dream in life,
Some people never have.
The gleaming beam,
He chases the stream of screams away.
He's my dad.

I stand strong

All
Knowing and loving continuously.
I wanted to be free,
So he set me free.
I wanted to be loved,
So he put the love inside of me.
The problems in my life,
The stress that goes on in my head
While I'm lying in my bed,
During my nights of restlessness,
He picks me up and hold's me on his breast.
Inside I can hear him.
All I have to do is confess in my consciousness,
Only for him to hear.
All the things he has done,
Make's me feel like I have wings.
Wings to soar.
Uncountable ways he has blessed me.
I stand strong upon the land of the weak.

God's Love

A collaborated work with Kizzy Nadel

I carry a pain around in my heart.
My brain feels hollow like.
Empty raindrop falling on a windowpane.
Conceding feelings I pray for.
Love bleeds through my skin.
I know I am forgiven.
I will proceed to him.
I will not let evil feed my greed.
The emptiness has left me with no way to see.
I wake up with it...
I take a breath with it...
I even fake a smile with it.
God's love saved me.
I feel pure with him.
He assured me that cured I'd be.
My past only he can see.
I think I will shout!!!!
GOD saved me.

Freedom

It's a feeling of prosperity.
Continuing a life long journey for acceptance of your self.
Freedom from poverty.
Chains and shackles,
Holds life by the faith.
Freedom
The willingness to get up,
Walk away and never look back.
The strength that give the power to know.

Soundness from my own mind.
Freedom
Faith,
That sounds so promising.
Refreshing,
Like summer rain in the morning.
Freedom
Keys to unlocking all life's secrets.
To fly high above the sky.
Ability to open my heart wide.
Freedom
Only with faith we can walk in freedom.
See in freedom.
Feel in freedom.
To just be free.

For Me

You saved me.
I honor the life you gave me.
I know you will never forsake me.
Because you have redeemed me.
You have foreseen the future.
I have been captured by your love.
You were sent from above for me to love.

Family

When I sit alone,
I often think of home.
That small thing I didn't no id miss,
I never envisioned ending up like this.
This is were I make a new start,
My family and I don't belong apart.

Eleanor Lee

Each day they grow,
I can make it ill just take it slow.
Support from family and friends,
Will soon lead the bad to an end.
I can do it,
The feelings are right.
This time I will make it no more I might.

Faith

When I sit still,
I try to unwind,
But unkind thoughts fly blind though my mind.
Trying to sort through my dying memories,
So I can grin and say,
There's always a better day.
To be able to lay back and pray,
That the ray of hope has not yet faded away.
Knowing that my gray days are far away.

To John

You've been in my life for many years!
We told each other all of our Dreams, thoughts, and fears.
A brother to me, you have been. A
brother like u is my best friend!
A brother like you, I have needed. A brother's
heart like yours is reason for succeeding.
I felt sorrow to see after all of that, you
are not such a gentle wind.
Life for me came to an end.
That's when I figured out you where not a
Reliable and trustworthy friend. Through the
abundance of time we shared together,

We together can manage hell's weather.
You neglected to tell me my sprit was dirty.
You never told me god could wash me.
My brother… You were, only sometimes I am sure! Help the spirits of our friends.
Tell them, God can mend them!
PLEASE!!!!!
Or God will send them to sit in hell next to me!!!

COLORS

My life is like a beautiful picture.
The hands of God are painting it.
I need for nothing.
God's colors.
Blue in the sky,
Like the blue in my eyes.
Brown on the ground,
Like the brown in my hair.
Red in the lips that speak his word.
God's colors.
Yellow for the fellowship when we gather.
Green for the keen intuition I have seen.
Orange for I have never had to forage.
Purple for the precious persistence that I posses.
White for the light that he creates.
Black for the things I don't lack.
Clear for the glory that he gave me.
I think His picture is complete.

Bright-Knights

Hero's of our country,
Deserve our prayers and blessings.
They fight to preserve the right life.

Those bright-knights save,
All men, children and wives.
With out them,
We wouldn't know what freedom is.
Don't just toss them aside,
Widen your eyes and hear their cries.
They sacrifice and become paralyzed,
So we can be free.
They are heroes without their bravery,
WE would be nothing.
Our spirits,
Would be captivated in slavery.
WE have forgotten how free we are.
WE act like rotten children.
The profound feeling surrounds me.
I think it is time,
We stand up and say,
You are appreciated.
Thank you

Broken No more

Dedicated To Missy & Hank

The hurt they felt,
Before there devoted spirits found each other.
Their discouraged spirits started to disappear,
Until their delicate ears clearly heard each other's fears.
The lies they heard.
Their blind eyes
Seen through each other's unwise disguise.
Loneliness,
Started to rape and render the most of them,
Before their tasteful kisses had each other mesmerized.
With each other,

They soar and touch the sky.
It's stunning love,
Blessed from above,
Like a morning dove,
For many years they prayed,
For a little faithfulness.
Then God sent them a hero,
Compassion completely consumes the worst of them.
The hollow hole in them...
Is now filled with love.
The one,
Their life,
Their blessings have healed them with love.
Now they're broken no more.

Innocents of a Child

The eyes of a child are the keys to there soul.
Their hearts are soft for others.
Their imaginations run wild.
They know nothing of the bad they do.
Innocents of a child.
Love they so desperately want to share.
Your touch they long to feel.
The reality they know nothing of.
How easy it is to rewrite their fragile minds.
Innocents of a child.
The smile they always keep.
The shelter they seek.
The fun they desire to have.
The help they need to give.
Ways they make life seem so simple.
The way they feel secure when you are with them.
Innocent of a child.

The way their tears shatter your heart.
They always know something is wrong no matter
how hard you try to hide it.
Help save the innocents.

A National Outcry

Our nation is crying out loud.
People are sick and dieing.
We are doing nothing,
Denying the loss of our john doe's.
Baby's being abandoned,
The neglect.
Projected feelings of a perfect
    place laced with death.
The hot breathe of the devil's sigh.
Obsession is increasing!
Deception is rising!
Artificial lights in dark holes?
That doesn't seam right.
A sight so cold we are forced to cover it up.
Pretending we don't see it,
Feel it,
See it.
A hidden feeling of disparity.
As controversy lays in there minds;
Questions...
Why
What happened?
People that were supposed to love them the most didn't.
Why live?
Rezones for suicide.
Cardboard hotel.
Trashcan diners.

Reminds us of why we don't look.
We don't hear their cries.
Glance away from their signs for help.
'They did it to them selves".
Our excuses.
Justification.
We don't care.
A satisfaction in ourselves by seeing them.
It's a new story everyday.

III Remember

Worthy is your name.
You came to the cross,
To bare my shame.
I never new before you cared.
I was truly scared.
My life was is pieces,
You came and repaired it.
When I look in side of me,
You are all I see.
You are The Son of God,
But yet you still died for me.
Now I truly believe.
I will remember,
How you died.
I will remember,
How you lived.
I have been set free,
A Blessing from you and sent to me.
The gift of eternal life you bring.

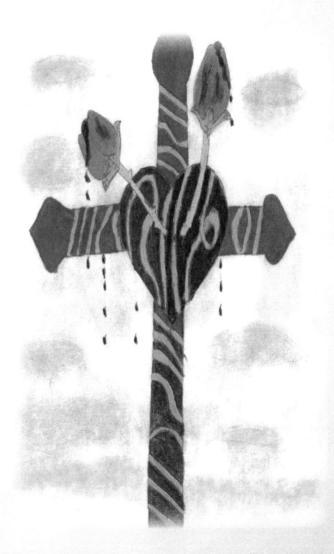

Eleanor Lee

Cluttered Thoughts

Thousands of people around me,
But still I feel alone.
Maybe I am forgotten.
Bound by destiny's twisted game of love.
The mysteries lay deep in time,
As deep as the never-ending mind.
Rocky waters of wilting and weary will.
Seeking answer unknown to there surgically sequenced souls.
Sounds sounding load,
Like the dreadful cries of Pandora's now none fate.
The shadow I walk with late at night.
An unknown being I long for.
Great graciousness of the unknown.
Ruff and tuff stuff I've sucked up and suppressed deep inside.
Broken thoughts,
They bind my mind in a kind and kindred way.
Gently lay on my pillow to forever stay awake.
Cleaver trick it take to taunt the tedious feeling away.
Still I pray day by day
To surly break this reckless chain.
As I lay still my soul remains calm.
I try to fight the feeling my body over doses on.
Delirious dilutions pray on my brain,
Diligent ways remain inconclusive as to how long they will stay.
Searching for something to satisfy my ferocious hunger.
A tender new start is needed.
My soul and spirit have pleaded repeatedly,
Concededly I have ignored its cry.
Fear of completely seeing the utterly inevitable end.
Time to tend to my spirit.
Listen and hear the fear start to completely disappear.
Never to reappear in my mind again.

Truth

Abominations searching for truth,
Pursuing an idea full of emptiness.
Failing so badly they feels disabled;
Hearts incapable of feeling love.
The picture perfect principle
For impeccable peace.
A comforting yet undecipherable feeling of fierce fullness.
Subsided and still waters a rise feeling from engraved suffering.
They will fade away as long as I pray
Day by day to keep me from my weary ways.
The rain slows to a light sprinkle now I can finally see the stars twinkle.
The clouds thin and start to disappear and the sky becomes clear.
My skin is now dry,
Were tears used to drain the stains of sin from the core of my mentally twisted mind?
An icy cold feeling rolls strongly over me:
Slowly grimy greed retrieves me from innocence.
IV completed pleading and treating my self-unfair.
The stairs and glairs that gleam from their eyes
Burn through me like fire through ice.

Power Trip

Perishing persons of power.
Diminishing the disaster of politics.
Promiscuous presidents acting like predators.
Kings with rings that sing about nothing but ching ching.
Mayors that don't care about the rare situations we face.
The place where our races awaits the taste of true life.

Love and Fate

A dream desired by my heart,
But shunned apart by my soul.
A torn heart stunned by love.
My soul knows he's a grim myth.
My mind has chose to grow away.
A distant flow grows faster.
Disaster comes closer and closer.
Displeasure buries its self-deep inside of me.
A treasure from fate tells me he is not true.
The view through my heart says he can be better,
Fate tells me I don't have time to weight and find out.

Survivor

A destiny or a choice.
You can choose to loose,
Or perceive to succeed.
Just one move can define,
The winners from the losers.
Be his survivor.
You determine your fate.
You can weep your wrong,
Or sing a victory song.
Everyone has a place where they belong.
Be his survivor.
I promise,
It won't be long till you see you life come undone.
My spirit won that battle.
Not the devil.
Be his survivor.
Decisions sometimes rattle my brain.
A decision mad quick,

Might send your life to the dark abyss.
If you think first,
It's not all ways the worst that happens.
Be his survivor.
When I see my strength start to disappear,
I no that the devil is in my head.
My heart gets hot,
My face gets red.
Than I know that evil is pulling at me.
BE his survivor.
In my heart and head,
It's an eternal race.
Soon the devil will be frantic.
Soon I will not fear him.
When my days are done,
I will be his survivor.

Released.

An unlocked window will set you free.
What does it do for your spirit?
Everyone has felt confined,
Jailed in his or her own personal prison.
Bound by weeping worriers,
Suppressed spirits.
Because of our sinful humanity we convict our selves.
From these walls is our only freedom.
Release these chains we bind our selves with,
Set our spirits free.

Seeker

A seeker seeking the sought.
Feeling of Beastliness and...
Bullheadedness scavenges my body.
Transportation is needed.
Cheerlessness to cheerfulness.
Carelessness to carefulness.
There's a place in my heart,
That is still left,
Untouched and un-dirtied.
I'm still listening for answers to questions I've asked.
Devil tries to trick me.
Levels rise around me.
Time to put the hardship behind me.
Blind crime reminds me of truth.

Sensational Love

Disfigured romance,
Arousing feelings of clothing coming of.
A royal stream of loyal touches.
Righteousness for forgetfulness.
It's sensational love.
Reminding me over and over,
The fulfillment of loves sacrifice.
Love overflowing like condensation.
Assurance for endurance that last all night.
Sensational love.
My heart burns with the feeling of a brand new sun.
The night goes on like the legacy of King Kong.
Belonging feelings for the taste of love.

The Burn

Memories with desire,
My feelings need to rest.
Old memories from the past play over in my head.
Leaves no room for spectacular days.
Why do they hit so hard when I am sleeping?
Or laying in my bed weeping.
I find myself listening to the music,
Inviting greetings from pain.
Sorrow flows through my brain,
Like insane tidal waves.
Just like stains of red wine on my page.
Rage that builds and burns in my body,
Leaves me with no way out,
Except to look toward something godly.

Secret Love

No more prideful tears.
No more repetitive and collective fears.
Passion is raiding my body.
It's what gives me a godly glow.
It's the substance that brakes up,
The harden parts of my cold heart.
The warmth unfolds the ice crystals.
The piano in my head begins to sound,
My heart thinks love is found.
It's time to stop deceiving my heart.
I've been driven to the point of no return.
Just to learn that love is not discerned.
God showed me the light.
So now I stand stern,
In a subconscious place that still burns.

My lips and tong are ready for a taste.
To see true loves sweet and perfect face.
, AS my heart begins to race,
It slows at the same pace.
The blood rushes to my face.
My hips and thighs feel the rhythm.
My breast go blush,
For anticipation of that tender touch.
The over whelming feeling fills me fast,
Like fierce fall winds.
Seduction that pierces through the cement I've carefully laid
My body percussion clumsily pushes down,
The polls that hold my walls in place.
Feelings of love seep deeper and deeper,
To my heart the keeper.
My soul burns of lust.
My mind lingers on that contentious must.
I'm that just vessel for secret love.
A secret love that may never be,
Until the lord shows me truth,
Then I will see.
I will see secret loves face,
That face will also see me.
When that face meets the perfection,
Of time is when he will only see me.
His skin so soft,
His touch so sweet,
I'm left longing from my head to my feet.
My weeping is seeping the street.
His submissive touch,
Lets a vibrant glow from his gloomy heart.
His yearn charges on like a theft in the night.
Getting stronger with every sight.
The more he tries to hide it the stronger it fights.
My silky skin forces him to touch ever so gently.

His sexual movement weighs on my mind,
Like a glow from a bright light.
I fight harder to suppress thoughts of him
I see that he is bound,
To a witch that tricks him.
She sucks the spirit out of him,
Like a parasite.
For I see the fire in him has faded.
He's a little further from his family.
The light that used to shine so bright in his eyes
Has got dimmer.
He is fading away no more glimmer.

Stand as Me

I stand as me,
With out you,
To be as free as the sea.
I stand as me,
I don't want to be you,
To be true to whom I am.
Just me,
It's truly overdue.

The Beginning

The hurt,
The pain,
The sacrifice.
When man becomes a deadly weapon,
A cross becomes a sacred memorable.
Hatless love that he gave,
He was not appreciated.
A life that thought about everyone but himself.

A fatherly brother that some no nothing of.
The crucifixion,
The emptiness we feel through his death.
We lost precious love.
The powerful loss of greatness.
A sinless being with perfect love.
Now we regret our hands of hate.
He saves you like he saves me.
The thanks,
The appreciation.
Your end gave us a new beginning.

Thrive To Shine

My eyes are open,
But they see nothing.
My body is awake,
But my mind is asleep.
My lungs are working,
But I am suffocating.
My legs are not broken,
But they have taken me nowhere.
My ears can hear,
But silence reigns,
My tongue cam taste,
But it all tastes the same.
My body is as artificial,
As my heart has become.
A spec in a large nothing-ness.
The light in me is fading.
The light struggles to shine,
But it is smothered my life.
A consistent persistence that has no confidents.
But my light still shines.

Feelings

My fear binds me down,
But no tears will come this time around,
I've found that special thing to hold on to.
That thing that makes the cold pass on.
My Little ray of freshness.
My baby girls
The feeling of falling on my face is rising.
How powerful the blow was isn't surprising.
I feel I have to hide myself,
Walk with the utmost stealth.
My fear is filling up hollow folds in my soul.
My cold nights are soon to grow.
But my freshness continues to chip ice away.
I find myself straying away.

Trust Me

Understanding,
Made my faith distend.
Faith blessed me with joy,
To makes my soul with stand sin.
When I start to fall you say,
"Stand tall and trust me".
Believe...
Even if I cant see you.
When I start to doubt you,
I see I can't live without you.
You always bring me back with two words.
"Trust me".
What does that mean?
I wonder!
Terrific truth

Rousing love
Unique relationship
Satisfying hunger
The blessing
Magnificent grace
everything I need
Trust me

Unknown Guidance

My strength,
I feel it begin to fade.
Now,
I am afraid.
I start to run,
Hiding myself from a healthy life.
My choices guiding me through great wealth.
Fear pushes me to the edge,
Failure forcing me to rear up.
Evil begins to sell.
Fear begins to propel.
Watching will become participating,
Participating will become experimenting.
Dieing will start.
Crying will never part.
Bones deteriorating,
Soul rearranging.
I need help.
My spirits full greed.
I'm lost.
It's cost me my independence.
Dependant on a drug.
I drop to my knees and begin to pray,
Help me stop,

I beg you please.
It lays on my mind till my day dies.
Why are you not here?
Why cannot hear you clear?
Why have ignored my fear?
The weight on my shoulders intensifies.
Evil sedates my soul,
Till I can't hear it no more.
Suddenly…
T feel cold shivers down my spine.
A bold and fierce,
Yet gentle voice,
I hear.
My child I am here,
Come near and lend me your ear.
I have never left you,
Let me be clear.
The weight you feel,
Is my spirit grounding you?
So you don't stray away
I held your hand even when you stopped holding mine.
I never left you,
It was you who turned your back on me.

Through The Worst

I can't always remember where I've been.
With in me he begins to mend.
With out him my life would end.
When I cry,
You wipe my tears,
Then tell me I have nothing to fear.
Those years I didn't have you,
I felt I would disappear.

When I knelt and found you,
I vowed I would live through you.
You are the food that feeds my hunger.
The wine that quenches my thirst.
You have always been there,
Always,
Through the worst.

Un-Perfect

An un-perfect self image.
A rejected reflection of my self-respect.
Collections of infections,
Embedded in the spirit.
A state longed for by all of us;
Reached by none.
Our flaws define us.
They make us who we are.
Theirs only one that has lived...
To see perfection.
We all carry a little piece of him in our spirits.
We all carry a little piece of perfect in our souls.

A Soul So Direr

Fatigue ness very bitter;
Wisdom drenched in clamminess.
Places of refuge become my prison.
Prison waters the seed of insanity in my head.
The misunderstood soul.
Even misunderstood by my mind's eye.
A soul so dyer
The feeling of rebuke by the world.
Here in my prison I sit,

Portrayed by the dark abyss of nothingness.
A soul so dyer
I need a vigorous hero.
My heart is in need of saving.
The zenith in my life is soon to come.
The eyes of god are in every place,
Watching every face.
With the want and willingness to distribute grace.
Grace for those soul so dyer.
It's time to pace my self,
Stealth will take me through the days of tomorrow.
Stocking my way through life,
Predator's potent feeling of a dissolute world.
Cunning.
Brave.
Cocksure.
I will posses these,
Till I meet my grave.
A dreadful light-mindedness falls over the world.
Beams of light dim in my world everyday.
I will pay for the sins.
Sins seem to direct my path.
Fear arises in my soul,
It leaves a cold emptiness filled with darkness.
It consumes me from my head to my feet.

What I Want In a Mother

Your mother you can turn to.
She always makes time to listen to you.
When you're sad and feeling down,
She always around.
She will sit and laugh and talk awhile.
You sometime realize how you resemble each other.

She's always around.
She thinks you are very special.
She your mother.

I've survived

I've survived the darkest days,
The coldest nights.
With you it feels so right.
Your eyes lights my day.
Your hands warm my nights.
Your presence lifts me off my feet,
Gives me nothing to weep
If you say,
You are mine,
Then my light will shine.
The sight of you,
Ignites a fire in me,
That takes me to greater heights
because you give strength.

Inferno

My love for him is red hot,
Like an inferno.
His love for me is eternal.
My past,
I hide it so no one knows.
But now,
I can't help but let it show.
Like an inferno.
The glow I have shines bright,
I give off my own light.
No more battle to fight,

I give them to him and he makes everything all right.
My sight can see the gleam of my blessings.
My loyalty now lies with him.
The only true royalty.
His love is impeccable.
I want to be inseparable from his love.
He shelters me from above.

Thank you for reading

**Any comments can be emailed directly to Eleanor Lee at
vuotorain@yahoo.com**

Printed in the United States
By Bookmasters